ALTERNATOR
BOOKS™

D-DAY
INVASION

Matt Doeden

Lerner Publications ◆ Minneapolis

Content consultant: Eric Juhnke, Professor of History, Briar Cliff University

Lerner Publications Company
A division of Lerner Publishing Group, Inc.
241 First Avenue North
Minneapolis, MN 55401 USA

For reading levels and more information, look up this title at www.lernerbooks.com.

Main body text set in Aptifer Slab LT Pro Regular 11.5/18.
Typeface provided by Linotype AG.

Library of Congress Cataloging-in-Publication Data

Names: Doeden, Matt, author.
Title: D-day invasion / Matt Doeden.
Description: Minneapolis : Lerner Publications, [2018] | Series: Heroes of World
    War II | Includes bibliographical references and index. | Audience: Grades
    4-6. | Audience: Ages 8-12. | Description based on print version record and CIP
    data provided by publisher; resource not viewed.
Identifiers: LCCN 2017009635 (print) | LCCN 2017010515 (ebook) |
    ISBN 9781512498158 (eb pdf) | ISBN 9781512486407 (lb : alk. paper)
Subjects: LCSH: World War, 1939-1945)—Campaigns)—France)—Normandy)—
    Juvenile literature. | Normandy (France)—History)—Juvenile literature.
Classification: LCC D756.5.N6 (ebook) | LCC D756.5.N6 D63 2018 (print) | DDC
    940.54/21421)—dc23

LC record available at https://lccn.loc.gov/2017009635

Manufactured in the United States of America
1-43464-33204-7/6/2017

TABLE OF CONTENTS

INTRODUCTION
WELCOME TO NORMANDY

Waves battered the shore as swarms of **amphibious assault vehicles** approached Omaha Beach in Normandy, France. It was June 6, 1944, at the height of World War II (1939–1945). The United States, Canada, and Britain of the **Allied forces** were launching a surprise attack on the German military that had invaded France in 1940. The day would become known as D-day.

Sergeant Thomas Valance of the US Army Rangers looked out at the beach, scanning for the enemy. He couldn't see anyone. Valance and the members of his company rushed down the ramp of the assault ship. Ocean water came up to Valance's knees, and waves slammed against his back.

Thousands of Allied troops, ships, and aircraft approached the beaches of Normandy on D-day to attack German forces.

Over the sound of the waves came the *pop-pop-pop* of rifle fire. Bullets rained down on the US soldiers. Valance raised his rifle and fired back.

American troops run onto Omaha Beach carrying all their gear and weapons.

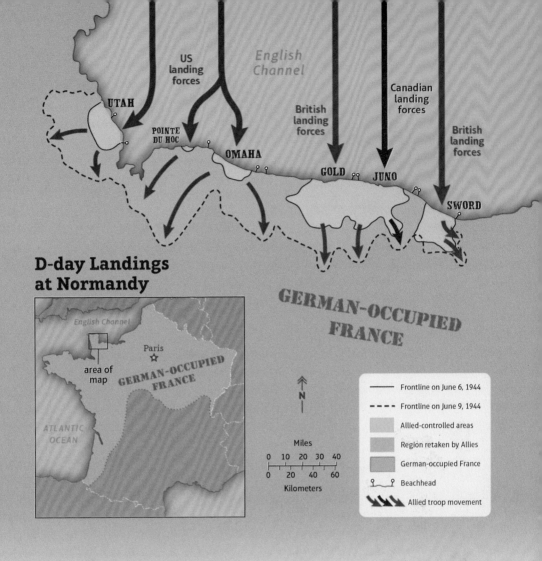

D-day Landings at Normandy

US landing forces

English Channel

Canadian landing forces

British landing forces

British landing forces

UTAH

POINTE DU HOC

OMAHA

GOLD

JUNO

SWORD

GERMAN-OCCUPIED FRANCE

English Channel

Paris ☆

area of map

GERMAN-OCCUPIED FRANCE

ATLANTIC OCEAN

Miles
0 10 20 30 40
0   20   40   60
Kilometers

Frontline on June 6, 1944
Frontline on June 9, 1944
Allied-controlled areas
Region retaken by Allies
German-occupied France
Beachhead
Allied troop movement

From the front, the enemy fire grew more intense. From behind, the waves continued to batter the troops. Valance abandoned much of his heavy gear. Another wave sent his body lurching forward. He threw his hand up to catch his balance.

American troops help one another onto a beach at Normandy.

That's when the bullet hit him. The shot broke his knuckle and passed through his palm. And Valance wasn't alone. Many others already had wounds far worse than his. "They're leaving us here to die like rats," shouted a private.

Bleeding, Valance marched on through the water. His rifle jammed, so he grabbed a smaller **carbine** and kept firing. Another shot struck him, this time in the thigh. Two more shots pierced his pack. Then one zipped right past his face, breaking the chin strap on his helmet. Valance staggered onto land and slumped to the ground.

As the battle raged around him, Valance watched the waves wash body after body onto the beach. The ocean turned red with blood.

Wreckage and debris cover Omaha Beach during the invasion.

CHAPTER 1
OPERATION OVERLORD

As World War II stretched into 1944, Germany and several other nations, known as the **Axis powers**, were growing weaker in western Europe. The stronger Allied forces knew they had to make their move.

Allied leaders started planning the largest **invasion** in military history—Operation Overlord. It would combine sea, air, and land power. The initial invasion would include about 156,000 troops, more than eleven thousand aircraft, and a huge naval assault force.

Allied ships and soldiers land at Omaha Beach on D-day.

EXERCISE TIGER

Training for the invasion took months, and it was all done in secret. But not everything went according to plan.

On April 28, 1944, medical assistant James Brown was part of a US training mission called Exercise Tiger. Troops were practicing the invasion on a beach in England late at night. But German torpedo boats spotted them. The Germans opened fire, hitting three of the landing ships. Brown struggled to treat the wounded as the ships went up in flames.

Following the Exercise Tiger mission, James Brown's heavily damaged ship returns to England.

"[The fire] was the only light we had," Brown said. "I could hear the German torpedo boats buzzing near us, but I couldn't see them. . . . Men were on fire jumping off our ship. To this day, I still see those men jumping with their gear on into the water."

MASSING FORCES

As D-day approached, Allied forces gathered in camps near the southern coast of England, just across the English Channel from France. Early on the morning of June 6, the sea filled with **landing craft**. Diana Granger, a member of Britain's Women's Royal Naval

Members of the Women's Royal Naval Service completed many jobs including operating radar equipment, forecasting weather, and planning naval operations.

The United States and Britain used a variety of landing craft during D-day. One kind was the Landing Craft Infantry (LCI). These ships had a very shallow draft, which meant that they did not go far beneath the surface of the water and could navigate very shallow coastal areas. The LCI could carry up to two hundred troops, who charged down a ramp into shallow water or directly onto the beach.

Service, was staying in a seaside hotel in Southsea, England. She watched as hundreds of thousands of men boarded their assault craft in the early morning hours. "We . . . woke up to the sound of military boots marching along the pavement across the road from the hotel," she said. "We knew the big day had started."

Military planes soared overhead as the fleet set sail. D-day had arrived.

CHAPTER 2
THE VIEW FROM ABOVE

In the weeks and months leading up to D-day, Allied pilots had bombed German airstrips and destroyed roads and railways to disrupt supply lines. This action weakened and scattered the German forces.

American planes fly over the French coast in an attack on German defenses before D-day.

During the battle, troops would rely on Allied airplanes for ground support. The Allied planes dropped supplies, blasted at German positions, and opened lines of attack for Allied troops.

FIRST WAVE

The invasion really began late on the night of June 5. At 9:50 p.m., a fleet of C-47 transport planes took off from England. Each plane was filled with twelve or more US **paratroopers**. Many also towed CG-4 Hadrians. These gliders with no engines could carry up to fifteen troops each.

US paratroopers prepare to jump from a plane in France.

Three D-day C-47s fly in formation during a demonstration in 2014.

Thirty-three-year-old American pilot Joel Crouch led the way for a V-shaped formation of C-47s. Crouch and the other pilots battled terrible flying conditions. Strong winds and rain battered the planes. The paratroopers Crouch carried knew that their mission was extremely dangerous. Yet the pilot later reported that the men sang the whole way.

BOMBS AWAY

Early on the morning of June 6, Allied bombers took to the skies. Captain Hale Bennett was one of the last to drop his bombs before the invasion began. Normally, his B-26 Marauder dropped its bombs from 10,000 feet (3,048 m) or higher. But cloud cover forced the bombers to go much lower—right into the range of enemy fire.

Bennett's B-26 dipped below 1,000 feet (305 m). He was right on top of the action. Debris from explosions flew all around his aircraft. He managed to avoid it and dropped his bombs just two minutes before the US troops hit the ground. He and his squadron turned and headed back to England to reload and refuel. Then it was on to another bombing run.

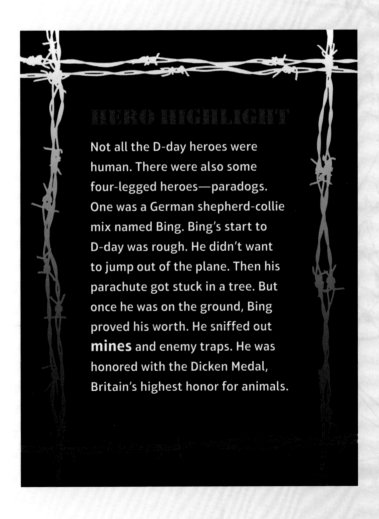

HERO HIGHLIGHT

Not all the D-day heroes were human. There were also some four-legged heroes—paradogs. One was a German shepherd-collie mix named Bing. Bing's start to D-day was rough. He didn't want to jump out of the plane. Then his parachute got stuck in a tree. But once he was on the ground, Bing proved his worth. He sniffed out **mines** and enemy traps. He was honored with the Dicken Medal, Britain's highest honor for animals.

CHAPTER 3
STORMING THE BEACH

The fighting on D-day started before the Allied invasion force ever set foot on land. The Germans had not known exactly when or where an attack would come. But their experts were sure that one was coming. They figured out where the Allies were likely to attack and set up defensive positions along 50 miles (80 km) of the coast. The enemy watched and waited as the fleet of Allied landing craft cut through the choppy water.

German troops lined the beaches at Normandy with barbed wire and wooden structures to slow down the Allied forces.

First Lieutenant Jimmie W. Monteith led a unit of fifty-one men. They were under fire from the moment they stepped off their landing craft into 3 feet (1 m) of cold water. Monteith dove underwater as shots rang out. He led his men toward the beach in a zigzag pattern, trying to avoid enemy fire. By the time they reached land, more than half the unit had been killed. Yet Monteith rallied his remaining troops and led an assault through an enemy minefield. He later died in the battle.

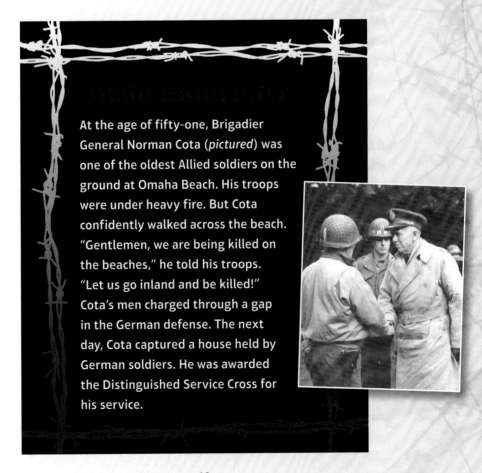

At the age of fifty-one, Brigadier General Norman Cota (*pictured*) was one of the oldest Allied soldiers on the ground at Omaha Beach. His troops were under heavy fire. But Cota confidently walked across the beach. "Gentlemen, we are being killed on the beaches," he told his troops. "Let us go inland and be killed!" Cota's men charged through a gap in the German defense. The next day, Cota captured a house held by German soldiers. He was awarded the Distinguished Service Cross for his service.

Following the invasion, American troops move through a destroyed town near the beach.

THE BATTLE DRAGS ON

As the soldiers fought their way onto the shore, larger landing craft delivered Allied tanks to the beach. Blasts from their big guns rocked the shore. Marie-Louise Osmont lived in a house overlooking the beach. She and her family crouched in a corner of their home as the battle raged on. That evening they went out to see the destruction.

"An airplane or tank shell has exploded on the paving in [the neighbor's] kitchen at the corner of the stairs, and the whole interior of the room is devastated," Osmont reported. "The big clock, dishes, cooking equipment, walls, everything is riddled with holes, the dishes in broken pieces, as are almost all the windowpanes."

D-day marked the start of the battle. Some of the war's most intense fighting took place that day. But D-day was far from the end of it. The Allies struggled just to gain a foothold. The actual invasion of Normandy would take more than a month. Over that time, the Allies landed more than one million troops.

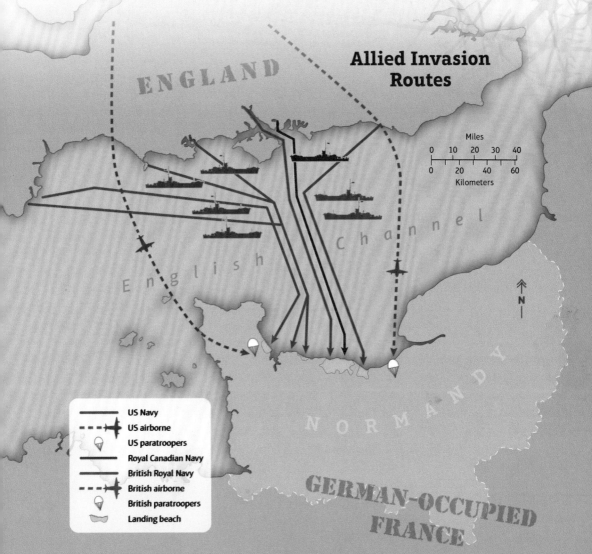

ENGLAND

Allied Invasion Routes

Miles
0   10   20   30   40

0   20   40   60
Kilometers

C h a n n e l

E n g l i s h

N

US Navy
US airborne
US paratroopers
Royal Canadian Navy
British Royal Navy
British airborne
British paratroopers
Landing beach

N O R M A N D Y

GERMAN-OCCUPIED
FRANCE

CHAPTER 4
CASUALTIES OF WAR

By the end of June, the Allies had gained control of Normandy. It was a crippling blow for the Germans. The Allies had broken the enemy's hold on western Europe and started their march toward Germany.

An American tank moves past a destroyed German tank during the invasion.

A group of US army nurses takes a lunch break outside a field hospital at Normandy in June 1944.

TENDING THE WOUNDED

The cost of victory was staggering. Thousands of Allied and enemy soldiers had been killed. More were wounded. Twenty-two-year-old Phyllis Henninger of Scotland worked as a nurse at a field hospital on the beach. The hospital didn't have nearly enough beds.

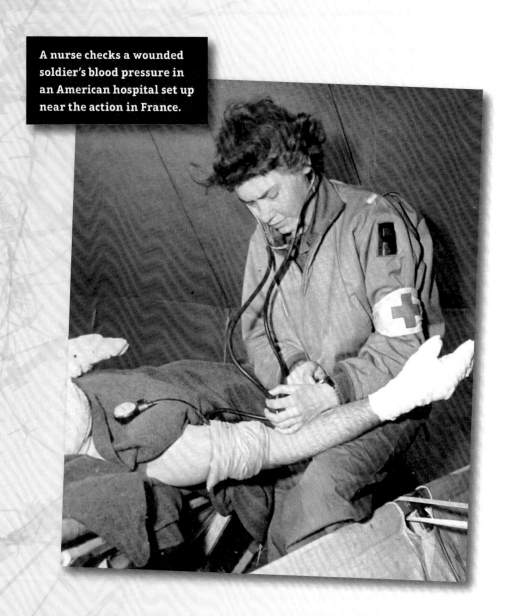

Henninger and the other nurses had to step over patients who were lying on the floor. The nurses sterilized syringes and other medical equipment in a boiling pot of water.

A new wonder drug called penicillin saved the lives of countless soldiers wounded on D-day. Penicillin was first used as an **antibiotic** in 1942. Before its development, infections such as gangrene were incurable. Amputation of an infected limb was the most common treatment. But penicillin fought off bacteria at the cellular level. It saved lives and limbs for soldiers on both sides of the war and became a staple of medicine for decades.

Allied soldiers also ended up in enemy hospitals. American soldier Robert Levine woke up in a German field hospital. A German doctor told him his wounded leg would be amputated. Then the doctor noticed the letter *H* on Levine's dog tags. The letter indicated that Levine was Jewish. The German Nazis were killing

Jews all over Europe. Levine feared that he would be killed too. But when Levine woke again, both his leg and his dog tags were gone. The doctor had hidden Levine's identity to save his life.

PRISONERS OF WAR

Other soldiers ended up in the hands of the enemy. Prisoners of war (POWs) were often treated harshly. Most were held until after the war ended almost a year later.

Reggie Salisbury was captured shortly after the invasion. German guards forced him and about fifteen others to march across France into Belgium. He was crammed into a filthy boxcar, questioned, beaten, and imprisoned. Salisbury and other POWs were forced to work and were given very little food. When he was finally rescued, Salisbury's weight had gone from 160 pounds (73 kg) to just 92 pounds (42 kg).

D-day was a victory for the Allies. One of the largest operations in military history, it turned the tide of the war. But it came at a terrible cost in lives. The stories of those who survived it can only give us a glimpse into the horrors of war.

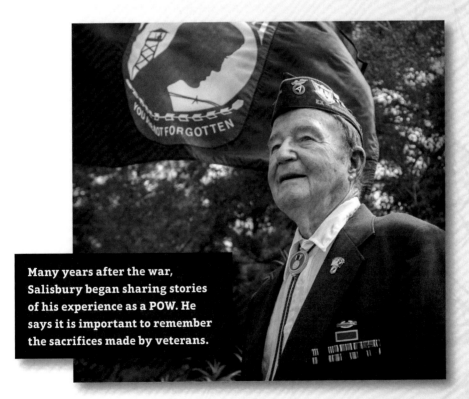

Many years after the war, Salisbury began sharing stories of his experience as a POW. He says it is important to remember the sacrifices made by veterans.

TIMELINE

September 1, 1939	The German Nazis invade Poland. World War II begins.
June 14, 1940	German forces invade Paris, France.
August 1943	The plan to invade France is first formed during a meeting with British prime minister Winston Churchill, US president Franklin Delano Roosevelt, and Canadian prime minister William Lyon Mackenzie King.
April 28, 1944	Exercise Tiger, a training mission, ends in disaster after German torpedo boats fire on Allied ships, destroying four of them and killing 749 men.
May 1944	General Dwight Eisenhower chooses June 5 as the date of the invasion. (It is later pushed back one day due to bad weather.)
June 5, 1944	The invasion fleet leaves England, and Allied planes begin dropping paratroopers into France.

June 6, 1944	The invasion begins. Early in the morning, landing craft drop off the first wave of Allied troops.
August 25, 1944	Allied forces free Paris from German control.
May 7, 1945	Germany formally surrenders, ending the European campaign of World War II.

SOURCE NOTES

8 "Voices of D-day: Thomas Valance," *PBS.org*, accessed February 2, 2017, http://www.pbs.org/wgbh/amex/dday/sfeature/sf_voices_04.html.

12 Dominique Debucquoy-Dodley, "Secret D-day Training Mission Cost Hundreds of Lives," *CNN.com*, June 6, 2014, http://www.cnn.com/2014/06/05/world/europe/D-day-training-mission.

13 "Memories of D-day: Preparing for D-day," D-day Museum & Overlord Embroidery, accessed February 9, 2017, http://www.ddaymuseum.co.uk/D-day/memories-of-D-day-preparing-for-D-day.

19 "Norman Cota, Overlooked Hero of D-day (and the Next)," New England Historical Society, accessed February 14, 2017, http://www.newenglandhistoricalsociety.com/norman-cota-overlooked-hero-D-day-next-day.

20 "Invasion of Normandy, June 6, 1944: A Civilian's View," *EyeWitness to History.com*, accessed February 14, 2017, http://www.eyewitnesstohistory.com/dday.htm.

GLOSSARY

Allied forces: the nations that fought against the Axis powers during World War II. The Allies included the United States, Britain, Canada, Russia, and others.

amphibious assault vehicles: military ships designed to carry troops to shore

antibiotic: a drug used to fight bacterial infections

Axis powers: the nations that fought against the Allied forces during World War II. They included Germany, Italy, and Japan.

carbine: a light automatic rifle

invasion: a military operation designed to take territory held by an enemy

landing craft: a ship or boat designed to deliver troops to land

mines: small explosives used either at or below the ground or water level

paratroopers: members of the military who use parachutes to drop into hard-to-reach areas

Further Information

BBC: World War II
http://www.bbc.co.uk/schools/primaryhistory/world_war2

Capek, Michael. *The D-day Invasion of Normandy.* Minneapolis: Abdo, 2016.

Drez, Ronald J. *Remember D-day: The Plan, the Invasion, Survivor Stories.* Washington, DC: National Geographic Books, 2015.

Ducksters: World War II
http://www.ducksters.com/history/world_war_ii

Kallen, Stuart A. *World War II Spies and Secret Agents.* Minneapolis: Lerner Publications, 2018.

National Geographic Kids: Ten Facts about World War II
http://www.natgeokids.com/uk/discover/history/general-history/world-war-two

INDEX

PHOTO ACKNOWLEDGMENTS

The images in this book are used with the permission of: iStockphoto.com/akinshin (barbed wire backgrounds throughout); iStockphoto.com/ElementalImaging, p. 1 (camouflage background); US Navy Seabee Museum, pp. 4–5; National Archives/Photo by Cpt. Herman Wall, 165th Signal Photo Co., p. 6; © Laura Westlund/Independent Picture Service, pp. 7, 21; National Archives (SC190366), p. 8; National Archives (80-G-252558), p. 9; National Archives (SC 193082), p. 10; Navy Medicine/flickr.com , p. 11; Not Known NI Syndication/Newscom, pp. 12, 29 (left); Time Life Pictures/Getty Images, p. 13; Wikimedia Commons, pp. 14, 28; AP Photo/US Army Signal Corps, p. 15; © Alan Wilson/flickr.com (CC BY-SA 2.0), p. 16; iStock.com/aaron007 (wire frame), pp. 17, 19; Robert O. Bare Collection (COLL/150) at the Marine Corps Archives and Special Collections (CC BY 2.0), p. 18; National Archives (111-SC-194926), p. 19; Popperfoto/Getty Images, pp. 20, 22, 29 (right); AP Photo, p. 23; Universal Images Group/Getty Images, p. 24; Photo 12/Alamy Stock Photo, p. 25; Cindy Yamanaka/ZUMAPRESS/Newscom, p. 26; US Air Force Photo/Airman 1st Class Tom Brading, p. 27.

Cover: National Archives/Photo by Cpt. Herman Wall, 165th Signal Photo Co. (soldiers); © iStockphoto.com/akinshin (barbed wire background); © iStockphoto.com/ElementalImaging (camouflage background); © iStockphoto.com/MillefloreImages (flag background).